NAVY

Civilian to SAILOR

by Meish Goldish

Consultant: Fred Pushies
U.S. SOF Adviser

BEARPORT
PUBLISHING

New York, New York

Credits

Cover and Title Page, © U.S. Navy/Mass Communication Specialist 2nd Class Jennifer A. Villalovos; 4, © U.S. Air Force/Master Sgt. Brian Nickey; 5, © U.S. Air Force/Master Sgt. Brian Nickey; 6L, © U.S. Navy/Adam Wolfe; 6R, © U.S. Navy/Photographer's Mate 1st Class Michael A. Worner; 7, © U.S. Navy/Scott A. Thornbloom; 8, © Scott Olson/Getty Images; 9, © U.S. Navy/Journalist 1st Class Preston Keres; 10T, © U.S. Navy/Scott A. Thornbloom; 10B, © U.S. Air Force/Master Sgt. Brian Nickey; 11, © U.S. Navy/Chief Photographer's Mate Chris Desmond; 12T, U.S. Air Force/Master Sgt. Jerry Morrison; 12B, Ralf-Finn Hestoft/Corbis; 13, © U.S. Air Force/ Master Sgt. Jerry Morrison; 14, © Scott Olson/Getty Images; 15, © U.S. Navy/Scott A. Thornbloom; 16, © U.S. Navy/Scott A. Thornbloom; 17, © U.S. Navy/Scott A. Thornbloom; 18L, © U.S. Navy/Journalist 1st Class Brandan W. Schulze; 18R, © U.S. Navy/Photographer's Mate 1st Class James Hampshire; 19, © U.S. Navy/ Photographer's Mate 1st Class James Hampshire; 20T, © U.S. Air Force/Master Sgt. Jerry Morrison; 20B, © U.S. Navy/Scott A. Thornbloom; 21, © Tannen Maury/EPA/Corbis; 22, © Justin Sullivan/Getty Images.

Publisher: Kenn Goin
Senior Editor: Lisa Wiseman
Creative Director: Spencer Brinker
Design: Debrah Kaiser
Photo Researcher: Daniella Nilva

Library of Congress Cataloging-in-Publication Data

Goldish, Meish.
 Navy : civilian to sailor / by Meish Goldish.
   p. cm. — (Becoming a soldier)
 Includes bibliographical references and index.
 ISBN-13: 978-1-936088-14-0 (library binding)
 ISBN-10: 1-936088-14-2 (library binding)
 1. Sailors—Training of—United States—Juvenile literature. 2. Basic training (Military education)—United States—Juvenile literature. 3. United States. Navy—Military life—Juvenile literature. I. Title.
 V433.G65 2011
 359.5'40973—dc22
                              2010018475

For more information, write to Bearport Publishing Company, Inc., 101 Fifth Avenue, Suite 6R, New York, New York 10003. Printed in the United States of America in North Mankato, Minnesota.

022011
012411CGC

10 9 8 7 6 5 4 3 2

Contents

A Daring Rescue

A team of **recruits** was aboard a ship when suddenly a loud explosion followed by gunfire filled the air. One recruit fell to the floor, wounded. His worried teammates hurriedly put him on a stretcher. Then, in the darkness, they **maneuvered** the stretcher through narrow passageways and under objects such as fallen poles. After much effort, they finally found a safe location.

Navy recruits make their way through a narrow passageway as they try to help an injured teammate.

Were these recruits under enemy attack? No. Luckily, this was only a **military** training exercise aboard a fake ship, and no one was hurt. It was a great learning experience for recruits such as Adam Wolfe. It taught them what to do in case of an actual attack against a U.S. Navy ship.

Recruits pull their wounded teammate under a large pole to get him to safety.

The navy is the branch of the **armed forces** responsible for military operations on the seas.

Signing Up

As a navy recruit, Adam Wolfe welcomed the excitement of training exercises like the fake ship attack. Excitement is the reason he had **enlisted** in the U.S. Navy to begin with. He wanted to face challenging situations and come away a stronger person by dealing with them successfully.

Adam Wolfe joined the navy in order to improve himself, find adventure, and see the world.

Just like Adam, about 40,000 people enlist in the U.S. Navy each year.

After signing up with the navy in 2007, Adam reported to the Great Lakes Naval Training Center in Illinois. All male and female navy recruits go there for basic training, which is also known as boot camp. This difficult nine-week program helps **civilians** learn **seamanship** and other skills they will need in order to become sailors.

Female recruits receiving their new uniforms

During their first week of boot camp, navy recruits are **processed**. They receive uniforms, and both men and women get short haircuts. Recruits are also shown how to fold and store their clothing and make their beds according to strict navy rules.

Group Leaders

After being processed, recruits are placed into groups called **divisions**. Each division has about 80 members. The group is assigned a sleeping area in the **barracks** called a ship. Though men and women train in the same divisions, they don't room together.

A sleeping area such as this one may house up to 1,000 recruits.

At boot camp, a division often marches as a group so its members can learn to work together as a team.

Each division is led by a recruit division **commander**, or RDC. The commanders, who may be male or female, are strict leaders. They make sure their divisions work as a team and follow orders exactly as they are given. An RDC may yell at someone who makes a mistake, such as folding a shirt incorrectly. Often, recruits are punished by having to do many sets of sit-ups or push-ups.

This **RDC** watches as his division does jumping jacks as a punishment.

Getting Physical

In order to do their jobs well, sailors must be strong. To build up their strength during boot camp, recruits spend at least one hour a day, six days a week, on physical training. A typical training session consists of a 1.5-mile (2.4-km) run as well as many sets of push-ups and **curl-ups**. By the end of the hour, the recruits are tired and their muscles are sore, but they are stronger!

Recruits train hard to build their muscles.

Navy recruits used to be allowed to call "time out" if they felt the need for a break during physical training. Today, no time-outs are given in order to make the training extra tough.

Since sailors work on ships, which are filled with narrow passageways, they must be able to move around quickly and easily. Therefore, recruits do many exercises that increase their **flexibility**. For example, in one exercise they sit on the ground with their legs straight out in front of them. With toes pointed up, they lean forward and touch their feet with their fingers for at least one second.

Flexibility exercises help recruits move more easily on ships, especially in emergencies when every second counts.

All the physical training that recruits go through helps them prepare for a physical fitness test that they must pass in order to graduate from boot camp. For the test, men are required to run 1.5 miles (2.4 km) in under 12 minutes and 15 seconds. Women must run it in under 14 minutes and 45 seconds. Both men and women also must do 54 curl-ups within 2 minutes. Finally, men must complete 46 push-ups in 2 minutes, while women must complete 20 push-ups in the same amount of time.

In the Water

Since sailors serve their country at sea, knowing how to swim is very important for navy recruits. During boot camp, they practice their swimming skills every day, doing many **laps** around the pool. This dramatically builds up their arm and leg muscles. They also learn how to rescue other swimmers and pull them to safety.

Sailors must be able to swim in case a ship emergency leaves them in the water.

All recruits are taught life-saving skills.

Before they can graduate from boot camp, recruits have to pass a swimming test. They must jump into deep water from a platform that is five feet (1.5 m) high. Then they have to swim 50 yards (46 m)—that's about half the length of a football field! At this point, even though they are exhausted, the recruits must float in the water for five minutes.

Recruits jumping off a platform during their swimming test

Navy recruits don't need to know how to swim before they start boot camp. However, they must become good swimmers in order to graduate. Recruits who can't swim when they enter the navy receive extra lessons to help them develop their skills.

Ready, Aim, Fire!

At boot camp, recruits learn many important survival skills. One of the most important is how to protect themselves from enemies. Recruits train with three weapons: the M9 pistol, the M16 rifle, and a 12-**gauge** shotgun. Recruits are taught how to fire each weapon, and how to take them apart, clean, and reassemble them. Taking good care of a weapon insures that it will work properly when it's needed.

A recruit learns how to properly stand and hold an M9 pistol.

As part of their training, recruits also learn what to do in case of a terrorist attack aboard a ship. They are taught how to use their weapons as well as their hands to defend themselves. Their training is based on the navy's experience with actual attacks that have occurred on ships in the past.

Recruits practice firing their pistols.

Recruits promise to live according to the navy's three main values: honor, courage, and **commitment**.

Fighting Fires

During boot camp, recruits also learn what to do during a fire aboard a ship. They are taught how to **extinguish** a fire and escape from smoke-filled areas. Recruits learn that a fire emergency requires quick action. They need to master their firefighting skills because their lives as well as the lives of their fellow shipmates depend on it.

Recruits practice using a heavy hose to put out a fire.

During fire-training exercises, recruits wear special suits and masks to protect themselves from the dangerous heat, flames, and smoke. They learn to work as a team, using large, heavy hoses to spray water on the raging fire until it is completely out.

During boot camp, recruits learn everything they need to know to put out a fire that might occur while at sea.

The special masks that the recruits wear help them breathe while fighting fires in smoky areas.

Endings and Beginnings

Right after Battle Stations ends, recruits experience a proud moment together. For the past nine weeks, they've worn baseball caps that read RECRUIT. Now, they remove those caps and put on new ones that read NAVY. They are now officially sailors.

A female recruit waiting to receive her new hat

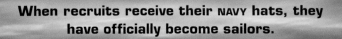

When recruits receive their NAVY hats, they have officially become sailors.

When recruits pass the Battle Stations exercise, they have completed basic training. At a special graduation ceremony, divisions march together for family and friends to show how they work together as a team. The ceremony doesn't mark an ending, however, but a beginning. The sailors will now attend a navy school for more education before they start their jobs. Sailors may work as anything from computer operators to cooks. No matter what their jobs are, all sailors serve proudly as members of the U.S. Navy.

Training after boot camp can last from several months to several years, depending on the type of job each sailor chooses to prepare for.

The new sailors proudly stand together at their graduation ceremony.

Preparing for the U.S. Navy

If you are interested in joining the U.S. Navy in the future, you can start preparing now by doing well in school, keeping your body in top physical shape, and being a responsible person. According to the U.S. government, the following rules also apply:

★ You must be between 17 and 34 years old.

★ You must be a U.S. citizen or a legal **alien** with permission to live in the country.

★ You should have a high school diploma. This is needed in order to join many of the navy programs that follow basic training.

★ Both men and women must be no shorter than 4 feet 10 inches (1.47 m) and no taller than 6 feet 6 inches (1.98 m).

★ You cannot have a serious criminal record.

★ You must pass a navy job skills test that measures your language, math, and science skills.

Glossary

alien (AY-lee-uhn) a person from a foreign country who now lives in another country

armed forces (ARMD FORSS-iz) the military groups a country uses to protect itself; in the United States these are the Army, the Navy, the Air Force, the Marines, and the Coast Guard

barracks (BA-ruhks) a building or buildings where soldiers live

capsizing (KAP-size-ing) turning over in the water

casualties (KAZH-oo-uhl-*teez*) people who are injured or killed in an accident, a disaster, or war

civilians (si-VIL-yuhnz) people who are not members of the armed forces

commander (kuh-MAN-duhr) someone in the armed forces who is in charge of a group of people

commitment (kuh-MIT-muhnt) a promise to do something

curls-ups (KURL-uhps) exercises like sit-ups, except that the knees are bent, and the arms are crossed over the chest

divisions (di-VIZH-uhnz) groups of U.S. Navy recruits who train together

enlisted (en-LIST-id) joined a branch of the armed forces

extinguish (ek-STING-gwish) to put out a flame or fire

flexibility (*flek*-suh-BIL-uh-tee) the ability to bend

gauge (GAYJ) the size of a gun barrel

laps (LAPS) more than one time around a swimming pool

maneuvered (muh-NOO-vurd) moved something carefully into a particular position

military (MIL-uh-*ter*-ee) having to do with soldiers or war

processed (PROSS-esst) to be put through an organized series of events, such as filling out paperwork and getting medical exams, before starting basic training

recruits (ri-KROOTS) people who have recently joined the armed forces

seamanship (SEE-muhn-ship) the skills needed to sail or work on a ship

shaft (SHAFT) a long, narrow passage that goes straight down

Index

Bibliography

Galanti, Donna Beckley. *Letters from Boot Camp: A Memoir of Navy Basic Training.* Bloomington, IN: iUniverse (2007).

Paradis, Adrian A. *Opportunities in Military Careers.* New York: McGraw-Hill (2006).

Read More

Kiland, Taylor Baldwin. *The U.S. Navy and Military Careers.* Berkeley Heights, NJ: Enslow (2008).

Yomtov, Nel. *Navy SEALs in Action.* New York: Bearport Publishing (2008).

Learn More Online

To learn more about the U.S. Navy, visit
www.bearportpublishing.com/BecomingaSoldier

About the Author

Meish Goldish has written more than 200 books for children. He lives in Brooklyn, New York.